Restoring The Sacred Masculine

A Journey to Healing and Wholeness

Hey this Journal Belongs to,

_____.

If you're not this person we ask that you kindly return it to its rightful owner! This Journal is very personal to the person it belongs to. You would not want someone reading about your story without your permission so be respectful and treat other as you want to be treated!

We Thank You In Advance!

Introduction

Welcome to a transformative journey of healing and self-discovery, one rooted in the powerful essence of masculine energy. This journal is designed as a guide and a companion as you embark on a path to reconnect with the traits of action, strength, and purpose that masculine energy embodies. Whether you seek to balance this energy within yourself or heal wounds associated with it, this journal provides a safe space to explore, reflect, and grow.

Masculine energy is about more than external strength or traditional roles—it is an internal force that drives us to take initiative, stand confidently in our truth, and pursue our purpose with clarity and determination. Yet, like all energy, when it is unbalanced or unhealed, it can manifest in ways that leave us feeling disconnected, rigid, or overwhelmed.

This journal invites you to dive deeper into what masculine energy means for you. Through prompts, exercises, and reflective questions, you will explore how this energy has shaped your life, where healing may be needed, and how you can cultivate a healthy expression of it. You will uncover patterns, release old narratives, and awaken a renewed sense of direction and empowerment.

As you move through these pages, remember that healing is a process—a journey, not a destination. Approach each entry with openness and curiosity, knowing that your masculine energy, when aligned with your true self, can be a source of profound strength, protection, and purpose in your life.

Let this journal be a sacred space for your healing and growth, as you work to harmonize your inner world and embrace the fullness of who you are.

Masculine Energy ☼:

Masculine energy is often described as a set of characteristics or qualities traditionally associated with masculinity or the male aspect of the human psyche. These traits are not exclusive to men and can be exhibited by individuals of any gender. Masculine energy is typically characterized by:

1. Action-Oriented: A focus on doing, achieving goals, and taking initiative.
2. Structure and Order: Emphasis on logic, discipline, and organization.
3. Strength and Assertiveness: Physical and mental resilience, confidence, and the ability to assert oneself in the world.
4. Independence: A desire for self-reliance and autonomy, often accompanied by a focus on personal responsibility.
5. Protection and Provision: The instinct to protect loved ones, provide for them, and ensure their well-being.
6. Direction and Purpose: A drive toward ambition, leadership, and purpose, with a clear sense of direction.

Masculine energy is often contrasted with feminine energy, which is more nurturing, receptive, and intuitive. Both energies exist in all people, and a healthy balance between the two is often considered ideal.

Section I: Getting Started

Your Why?

- Why did you choose to start this journal?

- What do you hope to achieve through this journey?

EXPECTATIONS

Healing from Pain and Reconnecting with Masculine Energy

When life's hardships cause wounds that distort one's connection to their masculine energy, healing becomes a journey of reclaiming strength, confidence, and purpose. Masculine energy, often characterized by traits like assertiveness, focus, protection, and action, can be overshadowed by pain, trauma, or societal conditioning. Here are ways to reconnect with and heal your masculine energy:

1. Acknowledge and Embrace Your Pain: Healing starts with acknowledging the hurt. It's okay to feel vulnerable. By confronting and embracing the pain, you allow yourself to understand its impact on your life and begin to release its hold over you.

2. Rebuild Confidence and Self-Worth: Pain can erode self-worth and make one doubt their strength. Practice self-compassion, set achievable goals, and celebrate small victories. Rebuilding confidence is essential to reconnect with your masculine energy.

3. Set Boundaries: A distorted masculine energy often manifests in difficulty with boundaries—either too rigid or too porous. Healthy boundaries protect your energy, allowing you to focus on growth while keeping negative influences at bay.

4. Channel Your Energy into Purpose: Masculine energy thrives on purpose and direction. Find activities or goals that give you a sense of meaning and progress. Whether it's in work, personal development, or relationships, having a clear direction can reignite your masculine drive.

5. Reconnect with Your Body: Physicality is deeply linked to masculine energy. Engage in physical activities like strength training, martial arts, or outdoor adventures. These not only strengthen your body but also ground your spirit, reconnecting you with your inner strength.

6. Balance Discipline with Flexibility: While masculine energy values discipline and order, flexibility is key to growth. Cultivate healthy routines, but be open to change and adaptation. This balance fosters resilience and adaptability in the face of challenges.

7. Practice Emotional Intelligence: Masculine energy isn't about suppressing emotions; it's about channeling them constructively. Learn to process and express your emotions in a healthy way. This can help in releasing suppressed anger, fear, or sadness, leading to emotional freedom.

8. Seek Support and Brotherhood: Surround yourself with positive role models or a supportive community that understands and respects the healing journey. Brotherhood and mentorship can be powerful tools for reclaiming your masculine energy, as you learn from others who have walked similar paths.

9. Spiritual Alignment: Whether through meditation, prayer, or connecting with nature, finding a spiritual practice can help align your masculine energy with your higher self. This spiritual grounding allows you to heal from within and regain a sense of purpose and direction.

Healing is a journey, not a destination. As you peel back the layers of pain and trauma, you'll reconnect with the essence of your masculine energy. With patience and persistence, you can emerge stronger, more aligned, and ready to step into the fullness of your power.

Personal Inventory

- Current state of mind: How do you feel today?

Cultivating Self-Awareness and Emotional Intelligence

Cultivating self-awareness and emotional intelligence while healing masculine energy involves a deep exploration of one's inner world, recognizing patterns, and understanding the emotional responses that have been conditioned by societal norms. Healing masculine energy requires breaking down the barriers of stoicism and detachment that often limit emotional expression, allowing vulnerability to emerge as a source of strength. This process fosters a balance between assertiveness and empathy, creating space for healing and growth. By embracing emotional intelligence, individuals can navigate their emotions with greater clarity, cultivating healthier relationships and a more harmonious sense of self.

- Key stressors in your life right now.

_____
_____
_____
_____
_____
_____

- Things that currently bring you joy.

_____
_____
_____
_____
_____
_____

Embracing Vulnerability: Source of Strength

It involves redefining what it means to be strong. Traditional views of masculinity often equate strength with stoicism and emotional restraint, but true strength lies in the courage to be open, to express emotions, and to connect with others on a deeper level. Vulnerability allows men to confront inner wounds, release suppressed feelings, and break free from limiting societal expectations. This authentic engagement with one's emotions fosters personal growth, resilience, and healthier relationships, ultimately transforming masculine energy into a balanced and empowered force.

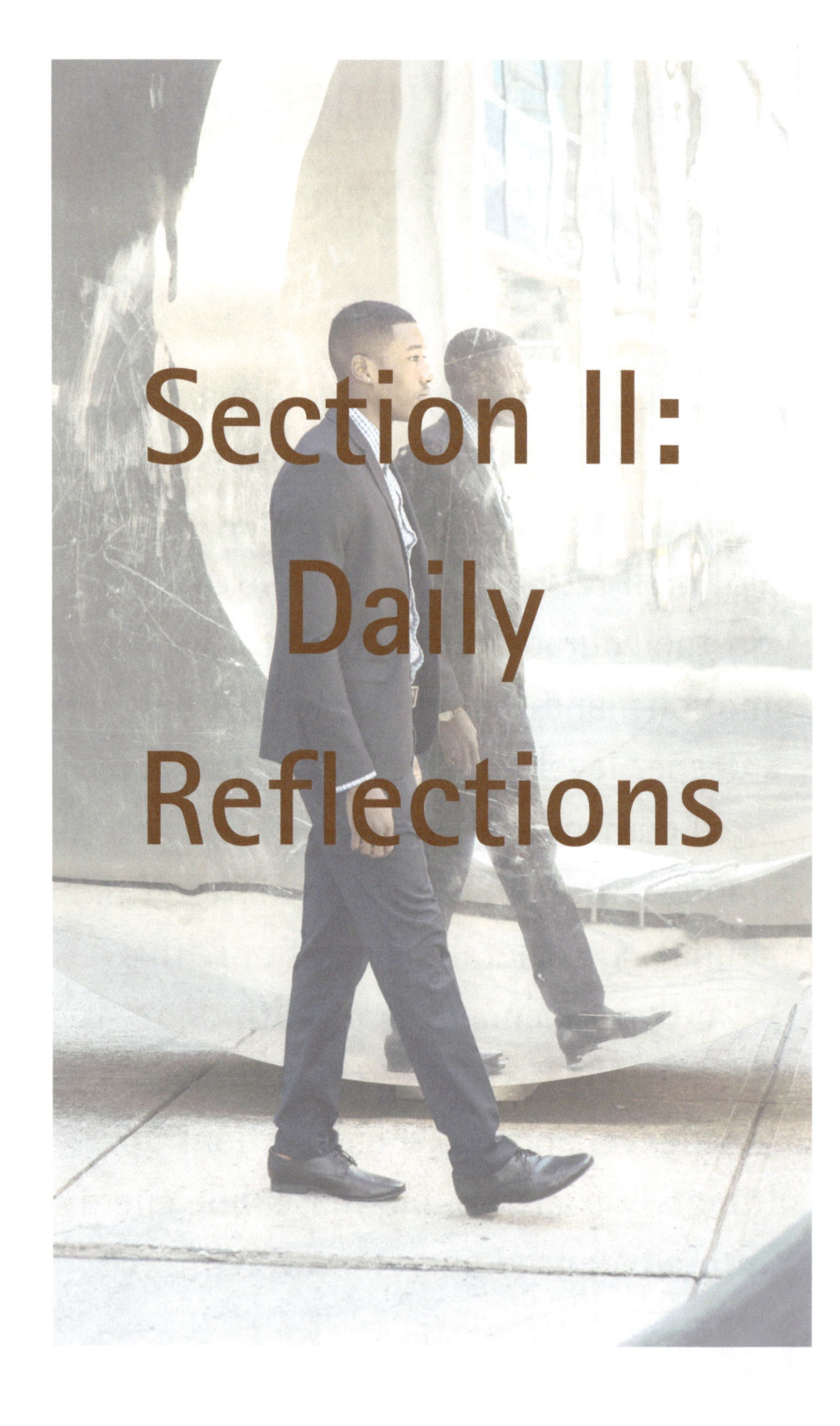

Section II: Daily Reflections

Importance of Daily Reflection

Daily reflection plays a crucial role in healing masculine energy by fostering self-awareness, emotional balance, and authentic strength. It allows individuals to pause and connect with their inner self, examining their thoughts, actions, and feelings without judgment. This practice encourages the release of societal pressures that often equate masculinity with constant productivity or emotional suppression. Through consistent reflection, men can nurture their emotional intelligence, cultivate empathy, and embrace vulnerability, which leads to a healthier, more holistic expression of masculine energy. Ultimately, daily reflection creates space for growth, healing, and a more balanced integration of masculine and feminine traits.

21 Days to A New You

Have you ever of the 21 Day Method?

• It involves committing to a daily practice of introspection for 21 consecutive days, allowing individuals to gradually build a habit of mindfulness and self-evaluation. Each day, participants take time to reflect on their thoughts, emotions, behaviors, and experiences, often through journaling, meditation, or quiet contemplation. This method leverages the concept that it takes about three weeks to form a habit, so by the end of the 21 days, self-reflection becomes an integral part of one's routine. Over time, this consistent practice can lead to deeper self-understanding, emotional healing, and the alignment of actions with personal values, ultimately fostering a more intentional and fulfilling life.

In this section we're going to focus on reflecting for 21 days!

Day 1

Date: _____

Morning Intention:

   - What is your main focus or intention for today? _____

   _____

Gratitude List:

   - Write down three things you are grateful for. _____

   _____

   _____

Positive Affirmations:

- List three affirmations to boost your confidence and positivity.

_____

_____

_____

Mood Tracker:

- Describe your mood in the morning, afternoon, and evening.

AM:
_____

Noon:
_____

PM:
_____

Daily Challenges:

- What obstacles did you face today?

_____

_____

_____

- How did you handle them?

_____

_____

_____

Self-Care Activity:

- What did you do to take care of yourself today?

_____

_____

_____

Evening Reflection:

- What went well today?

_____

_____

_____

_____

- What could have been better?

_____

_____

_____

_____

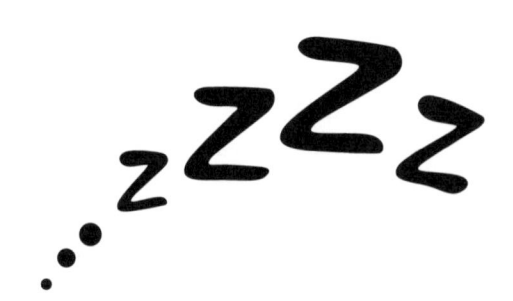

.·zZzz

Sleep Journal

- How well did you sleep last night?

_____

_____

_____

_____

- Any dreams or thoughts upon waking?

_____

_____

_____

_____

Day 2

Date: _____

Morning Intention:

   - What is your main focus or intention for today? _____

_____

Gratitude List:

   - Write down three things you are grateful for. _____

   _____

   _____

Positive Affirmations:

- List three affirmations to boost your confidence and positivity.

_____

_____

_____

Mood Tracker:

- Describe your mood in the morning, afternoon, and evening.

AM: _____

Noon: _____

PM: _____

STAY ACTIVE!

Daily Challenges:

- What obstacles did you face today?

_____

_____

_____

- How did you handle them?

_____

_____

_____

Self-Care Activity:

- What did you do to take care of yourself today?

_____

_____

_____

Evening Reflection:

- What went well today?

_____

_____

_____

_____

- What could have been better?

_____

_____

_____

_____

Sleep Journal

- How well did you sleep last night?

_____

_____

_____

_____

- Any dreams or thoughts upon waking?

_____

_____

_____

_____

Day 3

Date: _____

Morning Intention:

- What is your main focus or intention for today? _____
_____

Gratitude List:

- Write down three things you are grateful for. _____

_____

_____

Positive Affirmations:

- List three affirmations to boost your confidence and positivity.

_____

_____

_____

Mood Tracker:

- Describe your mood in the morning, afternoon, and evening.

AM: _____

Noon: _____

PM: _____

STAY ACTIVE!

Daily Challenges:

- What obstacles did you face today?

_____

_____

_____

- How did you handle them?

_____

_____

_____

Self-Care Activity:

- What did you do to take care of yourself today?

_____

_____

_____

Evening Reflection:

- What went well today?

_____

_____

_____

_____

- What could have been better?

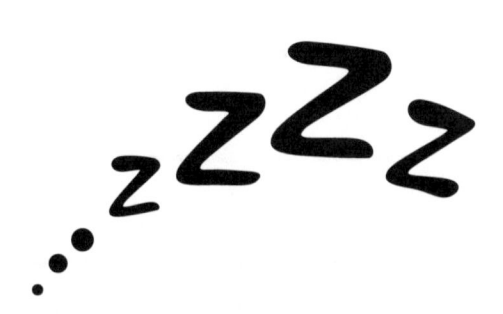

_____

_____

_____

_____

zZZz

Sleep Journal

- How well did you sleep last night?

_____

_____

_____

_____

- Any dreams or thoughts upon waking?

_____

_____

_____

_____

Day 4

Date: _____

Morning Intention:

- What is your main focus or intention for today? _____
_____

Gratitude List:

- Write down three things you are grateful for. _____

_____

_____

Positive Affirmations:

- List three affirmations to boost your confidence and positivity.

_____

_____

_____

Mood Tracker:

- Describe your mood in the morning, afternoon, and evening.

AM: _____

Noon: _____

PM: _____

Daily Challenges:

- What obstacles did you face today?

_____

_____

_____

- How did you handle them?

_____

_____

_____

Self-Care Activity:

- What did you do to take care of yourself today?

_____

_____

_____

Evening Reflection:

- What went well today?

_____

_____

_____

_____

- What could have been better?

_____

_____

_____

_____

zZZz

Sleep Journal

- How well did you sleep last night?

_____

_____

_____

_____

- Any dreams or thoughts upon waking?

_____

_____

_____

_____

Day 5

Date: _____

Morning Intention:

   - What is your main focus or intention for today? _____

_____

Gratitude List:

  - Write down three things you are grateful for. _____

        _____

        _____

Positive Affirmations:

- List three affirmations to boost your confidence and positivity.

_____

_____

_____

Mood Tracker:

- Describe your mood in the morning, afternoon, and evening.

AM:
_____

Noon:
_____

PM:
_____

STAY ACTIVE!

Daily Challenges:

- What obstacles did you face today?

_____

_____

_____

- How did you handle them?

_____

_____

_____

Self-Care Activity:

- What did you do to take care of yourself today?

_____

_____

_____

Evening Reflection:

- What went well today?

_____

_____

_____

_____

- What could have been better?

_____

_____

_____

_____

zZz

Sleep Journal

- How well did you sleep last night?

_____

_____

_____

_____

- Any dreams or thoughts upon waking?

_____

_____

_____

_____

Day 6

Date: _____

Morning Intention:

- What is your main focus or intention for today? _____

_____

Gratitude List:

- Write down three things you are grateful for. _____

_____

_____

Positive Affirmations:

- List three affirmations to boost your confidence and positivity.

_____

_____

_____

Mood Tracker:

- Describe your mood in the morning, afternoon, and evening.

AM: _____

Noon: _____

PM: _____

Daily Challenges:

- What obstacles did you face today?

_____

_____

_____

- How did you handle them?

_____

_____

_____

Self-Care Activity:

- What did you do to take care of yourself today?

_____

_____

_____

Evening Reflection:

- What went well today?

_____

_____

_____

_____

- What could have been better?

_____

_____

_____

_____

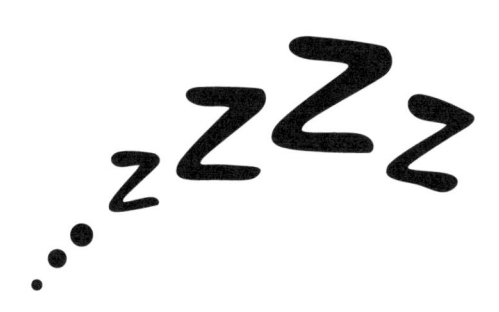

zZZz

Sleep Journal

- How well did you sleep last night?

_____

_____

_____

_____

- Any dreams or thoughts upon waking?

_____

_____

_____

_____

Day 7

Date: _____

Morning Intention:

   - What is your main focus or intention for today? _____
   _____

Gratitude List:

  - Write down three things you are grateful for. _____

   _____

   _____

Positive Affirmations:

- List three affirmations to boost your confidence and positivity.

_____

_____

_____

Mood Tracker:

- Describe your mood in the morning, afternoon, and evening.

AM:
_____

Noon:
_____

PM:
_____

STAY ACTIVE!

Daily Challenges:

- What obstacles did you face today?

_____
_____
_____

- How did you handle them?

_____
_____
_____

Self-Care Activity:

- What did you do to take care of yourself today?

_____
_____
_____

Evening Reflection:

- What went well today?

_____

_____

_____

_____

- What could have been better?

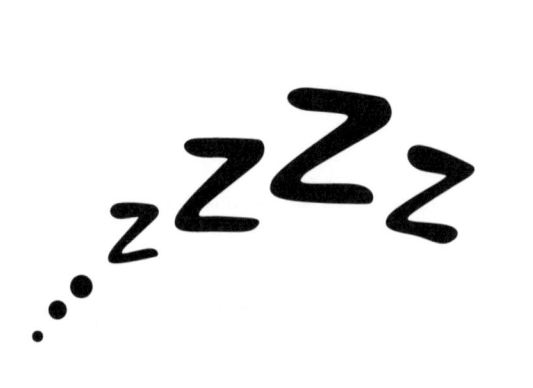

_____

_____

_____

_____

Sleep Journal

- How well did you sleep last night?

_____

_____

_____

_____

- Any dreams or thoughts upon waking?

_____

_____

_____

_____

Day 8

Date: _____

Morning Intention:

    - What is your main focus or intention for today? _____

_____

Gratitude List:

    - Write down three things you are grateful for. _____

_____

_____

Positive Affirmations:

- List three affirmations to boost your confidence and positivity.

_____

_____

_____

Mood Tracker:

- Describe your mood in the morning, afternoon, and evening.

AM: _____

Noon: _____

PM: _____

Daily Challenges:

- What obstacles did you face today?

_____

_____

_____

- How did you handle them?

_____

_____

_____

Self-Care Activity:

- What did you do to take care of yourself today?

_____

_____

_____

Evening Reflection:

- What went well today?

_____

_____

_____

_____

- What could have been better?

_____

_____

_____

_____

Sleep Journal

- How well did you sleep last night?

_____

_____

_____

_____

- Any dreams or thoughts upon waking?

_____

_____

_____

_____

Day 9

Date: _____

Morning Intention:

   - What is your main focus or intention for today? _____

_____

Gratitude List:

  - Write down three things you are grateful for. _____

    _____

    _____

Positive Affirmations:

- List three affirmations to boost your confidence and positivity.

_____

_____

_____

Mood Tracker:

- Describe your mood in the morning, afternoon, and evening.

AM:
_____

Noon:
_____

PM:
_____

Daily Challenges:

- What obstacles did you face today?

_____

_____

_____

- How did you handle them?

_____

_____

_____

Self-Care Activity:

- What did you do to take care of yourself today?

_____

_____

_____

Evening Reflection:

- What went well today?

_____

_____

_____

_____

- What could have been better?

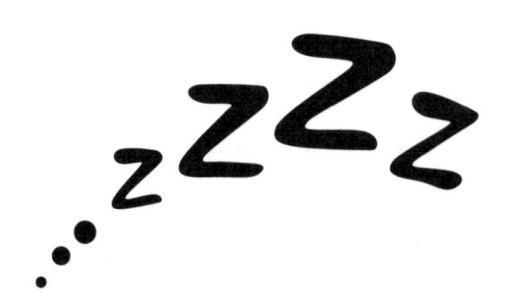

_____

_____

_____

_____

zZZz

Sleep Journal

- How well did you sleep last night?

_____
_____
_____
_____

- Any dreams or thoughts upon waking?

_____
_____
_____
_____

Day 10

Date: _____

Morning Intention:

    - What is your main focus or intention for today? _____

_____

Gratitude List:

    - Write down three things you are grateful for. _____

_____

_____

Positive Affirmations:

- List three affirmations to boost your confidence and positivity.

_____

_____

_____

Mood Tracker:

- Describe your mood in the morning, afternoon, and evening.

AM: _____

Noon: _____

PM: _____

STAY ACTIVE!

Daily Challenges:

- What obstacles did you face today?

_____

_____

_____

- How did you handle them?

_____

_____

_____

Self-Care Activity:

- What did you do to take care of yourself today?

_____

_____

_____

Evening Reflection:

- What went well today?

_____

_____

_____

_____

- What could have been better?

_____

_____

_____

_____

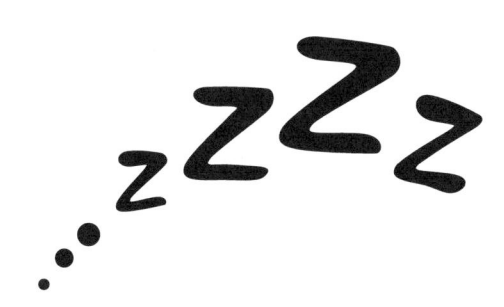

Sleep Journal

- How well did you sleep last night?

_____

_____

_____

_____

- Any dreams or thoughts upon waking?

_____

_____

_____

_____

Day 11

Date: _____

Morning Intention:

- What is your main focus or intention for today? _____
_____

Gratitude List:

- Write down three things you are grateful for. _____

_____

_____

Positive Affirmations:

- List three affirmations to boost your confidence and positivity.

_____

_____

_____

Mood Tracker:

- Describe your mood in the morning, afternoon, and evening.

AM: _____

Noon: _____

PM: _____

Daily Challenges:

- What obstacles did you face today?

_____

_____

_____

- How did you handle them?

_____

_____

_____

Self-Care Activity:

- What did you do to take care of yourself today?

_____

_____

_____

Evening Reflection:

- What went well today?

_____

_____

_____

_____

- What could have been better?

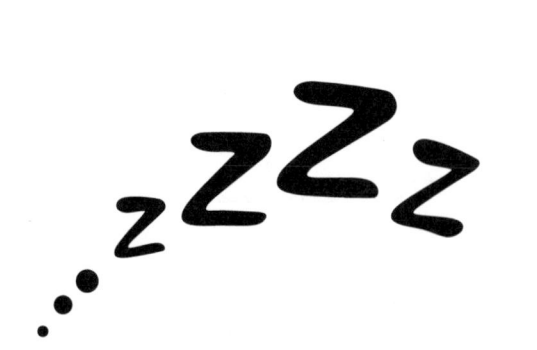

_____

_____

_____

_____

zZZz

Sleep Journal

- How well did you sleep last night?

_____

_____

_____

_____

- Any dreams or thoughts upon waking?

_____

_____

_____

_____

Day 12

Date: _____

Morning Intention:

- What is your main focus or intention for today? _____
_____

Gratitude List:

- Write down three things you are grateful for. _____

_____

_____

Positive Affirmations:

- List three affirmations to boost your confidence and positivity.

_____

_____

_____

Mood Tracker:

- Describe your mood in the morning, afternoon, and evening.

AM: _____

Noon: _____

PM: _____

Daily Challenges:

- What obstacles did you face today?

_____

_____

_____

- How did you handle them?

_____

_____

_____

Self-Care Activity:

- What did you do to take care of yourself today?

_____

_____

_____

Evening Reflection:

- What went well today?

_____

_____

_____

_____

- What could have been better?

_____

_____

_____

_____

zZZz

Sleep Journal

- How well did you sleep last night?

_____

_____

_____

_____

- Any dreams or thoughts upon waking?

_____

_____

_____

_____

Day 13

Date: _____

Morning Intention:

- What is your main focus or intention for today? _____

_____

Gratitude List:

- Write down three things you are grateful for. _____

_____

_____

Positive Affirmations:

- List three affirmations to boost your confidence and positivity.

_____

_____

_____

Mood Tracker:

- Describe your mood in the morning, afternoon, and evening.

AM:
_____

Noon:
_____

PM:
_____

STAY ACTIVE!

Daily Challenges:

- What obstacles did you face today?

_____

_____

_____

- How did you handle them?

_____

_____

_____

Self-Care Activity:

- What did you do to take care of yourself today?

_____

_____

_____

Evening Reflection:

- What went well today?

_____

_____

_____

_____

- What could have been better?

_____

_____

_____

_____

zZZz

Sleep Journal

- How well did you sleep last night?

_____

_____

_____

_____

- Any dreams or thoughts upon waking?

_____

_____

_____

_____

Day 14

Date: _____

Morning Intention:

- What is your main focus or intention for today? _____

_____

Gratitude List:

- Write down three things you are grateful for. _____

_____

_____

Positive Affirmations:

- List three affirmations to boost your confidence and positivity.

_____

_____

_____

Mood Tracker:

- Describe your mood in the morning, afternoon, and evening.

AM: _____

Noon: _____

PM: _____

Daily Challenges:

- What obstacles did you face today?

_____

_____

_____

- How did you handle them?

_____

_____

_____

Self-Care Activity:

- What did you do to take care of yourself today?

_____

_____

_____

Evening Reflection:

- What went well today?

_____

_____

_____

_____

- What could have been better?

_____

_____

_____

_____

Sleep Journal

- How well did you sleep last night?

_____

_____

_____

_____

- Any dreams or thoughts upon waking?

_____

_____

_____

_____

Day 15

Date: _____

Morning Intention:

- What is your main focus or intention for today? _____
_____

Gratitude List:

- Write down three things you are grateful for. _____

_____

_____

Positive Affirmations:

- List three affirmations to boost your confidence and positivity.

_____

_____

_____

Mood Tracker:

- Describe your mood in the morning, afternoon, and evening.

AM:
_____

Noon:
_____

PM:
_____

STAY ACTIVE!

Daily Challenges:

- What obstacles did you face today?

_____

_____

_____

- How did you handle them?

_____

_____

_____

Self-Care Activity:

- What did you do to take care of yourself today?

_____

_____

_____

Evening Reflection:

- What went well today?

_____

_____

_____

_____

- What could have been better?

_____

_____

_____

_____

zZZz

Sleep Journal

- How well did you sleep last night?

_____

_____

_____

_____

- Any dreams or thoughts upon waking?

_____

_____

_____

_____

Day 16

Date: _____

Morning Intention:

   - What is your main focus or intention for today? _____

_____

Gratitude List:

   - Write down three things you are grateful for. _____

_____

_____

Positive Affirmations:

- List three affirmations to boost your confidence and positivity.

_____

_____

_____

Mood Tracker:

- Describe your mood in the morning, afternoon, and evening.

AM: _____

Noon: _____

PM: _____

STAY ACTIVE!

Daily Challenges:

- What obstacles did you face today?

_____

_____

_____

- How did you handle them?

_____

_____

_____

Self-Care Activity:

- What did you do to take care of yourself today?

_____

_____

_____

Evening Reflection:

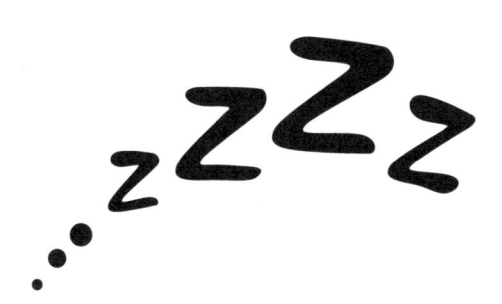

- What went well today?

_____

_____

_____

_____

- What could have been better?

_____

_____

_____

_____

zZZz

Sleep Journal

- How well did you sleep last night?

_____

_____

_____

_____

- Any dreams or thoughts upon waking?

_____

_____

_____

_____

Day 17

Date: _____

Morning Intention:

   - What is your main focus or intention for today? _____

_____

Gratitude List:

  - Write down three things you are grateful for. _____

                 _____

                 _____

Positive Affirmations:

- List three affirmations to boost your confidence and positivity.

_____

_____

_____

Mood Tracker:

- Describe your mood in the morning, afternoon, and evening.

AM: _____

Noon: _____

PM: _____

STAY ACTIVE!

Daily Challenges:

- What obstacles did you face today?

_____

_____

_____

- How did you handle them?

_____

_____

_____

Self-Care Activity:

- What did you do to take care of yourself today?

_____

_____

_____

Evening Reflection:

- What went well today?

_____

_____

_____

_____

- What could have been better?

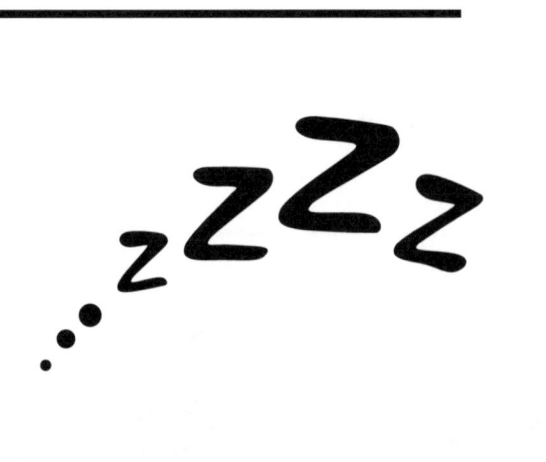

_____

_____

_____

_____

zZZz

Sleep Journal

- How well did you sleep last night?

_____

_____

_____

_____

- Any dreams or thoughts upon waking?

_____

_____

_____

_____

Day 18

Date: _____

Morning Intention:

   - What is your main focus or intention for today? _____

_____

Gratitude List:

   - Write down three things you are grateful for. _____

   _____

   _____

Positive Affirmations:

- List three affirmations to boost your confidence and positivity.

_____

_____

_____

Mood Tracker:

- Describe your mood in the morning, afternoon, and evening.

AM: _____

Noon: _____

PM: _____

Daily Challenges:

- What obstacles did you face today?

_____

_____

_____

- How did you handle them?

_____

_____

_____

Self-Care Activity:

- What did you do to take care of yourself today?

_____

_____

_____

Evening Reflection:

- What went well today?

_____

_____

_____

_____

- What could have been better?

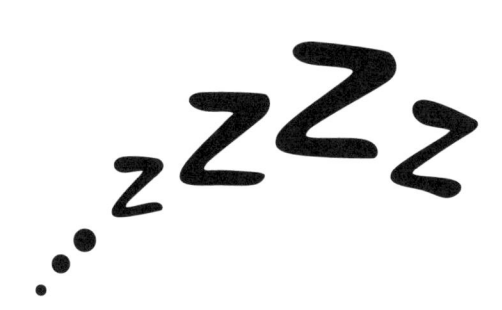

_____

_____

_____

_____

..zZZz

Sleep Journal

- How well did you sleep last night?

_____

_____

_____

_____

- Any dreams or thoughts upon waking?

_____

_____

_____

_____

Day 19

Date: _____

Morning Intention:

   - What is your main focus or intention for today? _____

_____

Gratitude List:

 - Write down three things you are grateful for. _____

    _____

    _____

Positive Affirmations:

- List three affirmations to boost your confidence and positivity.

_____

_____

_____

Mood Tracker:

- Describe your mood in the morning, afternoon, and evening.

AM: _____

Noon: _____

PM: _____

Daily Challenges:

- What obstacles did you face today?

_____

_____

_____

- How did you handle them?

_____

_____

_____

Self-Care Activity:

- What did you do to take care of yourself today?

_____

_____

_____

Evening Reflection:

- What went well today?

_____

_____

_____

_____

- What could have been better?

_____

_____

_____

_____

zzZz

Sleep Journal

- How well did you sleep last night?

_____

_____

_____

_____

- Any dreams or thoughts upon waking?

_____

_____

_____

_____

Day 20

Date: _____

Morning Intention:

   - What is your main focus or intention for today? _____
_____

Gratitude List:

   - Write down three things you are grateful for. _____

    _____

    _____

Positive Affirmations:

- List three affirmations to boost your confidence and positivity.

_____

_____

_____

Mood Tracker:

- Describe your mood in the morning, afternoon, and evening.

AM: _____

Noon: _____

PM: _____

Daily Challenges:

- What obstacles did you face today?

_____

_____

_____

- How did you handle them?

_____

_____

_____

Self-Care Activity:

- What did you do to take care of yourself today?

_____

_____

_____

Evening Reflection:

- What went well today?

_____

_____

_____

_____

- What could have been better?

_____

_____

_____

_____

zZzz

Sleep Journal

- How well did you sleep last night?

_____

_____

_____

_____

- Any dreams or thoughts upon waking?

_____

_____

_____

_____

Day 21

Date: _____

Morning Intention:

- What is your main focus or intention for today? _____
_____

Gratitude List:

- Write down three things you are grateful for. _____

_____

_____

Positive Affirmations:

- List three affirmations to boost your confidence and positivity.

_____

_____

_____

Mood Tracker:

- Describe your mood in the morning, afternoon, and evening.

AM: _____

Noon: _____

PM: _____

STAY ACTIVE!

Daily Challenges:

- What obstacles did you face today?

_____

_____

_____

- How did you handle them?

_____

_____

_____

Self-Care Activity:

- What did you do to take care of yourself today?

_____

_____

_____

Evening Reflection:

- What went well today?

_____

_____

_____

_____

- What could have been better?

_____

_____

_____

_____

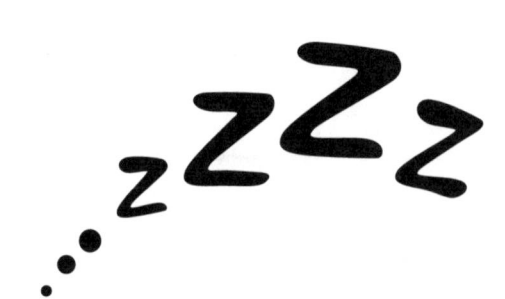

..zzZz

Sleep Journal

- How well did you sleep last night?

_____

_____

_____

_____

- Any dreams or thoughts upon waking?

_____

_____

_____

_____

How Do You Feel?

Section III: Weekly Check-Ins

Transitioning from Daily to Weekly Reflection

Transitioning from daily to weekly reflections can be a powerful way to restore and balance masculine energy. Daily reflections can sometimes feel overwhelming or routine, making it harder to see the broader patterns in your life. By shifting to a weekly practice, you allow space to step back and reflect on larger accomplishments, challenges, and areas for growth. This more strategic approach aligns with the masculine energy's natural tendency for long-term vision and goal-setting, offering a chance to recalibrate and take purposeful action. A weekly reflection can also help to prevent burnout by giving you time to recharge and refocus on what truly matters.

Week 1

Achievements:

- What were your major achievements this week?

Challenges:

- What challenges did you face this week?

_____
_____
_____
_____
_____

- How did you overcome them?

_____
_____
_____
_____
_____

Self-Reflection:

- What did you learn about yourself this week?

Goals for Next Week:

- What are your goals for the upcoming week?

_____

_____

_____

_____

_____

_____

_____

_____

_____

Week 2

Achievements:

- What were your major achievements this week?

Challenges:

- What challenges did you face this week?

_____
_____
_____
_____
_____
_____

- How did you overcome them?

_____
_____
_____
_____
_____

Self-Reflection:

- What did you learn about yourself this week?

Goals for Next Week:

- What are your goals for the upcoming week?

Week 3

Achievements:

- What were your major achievements this week?

Challenges:

- What challenges did you face this week?

_____

_____

_____

_____

_____

_____

- How did you overcome them?

_____

_____

_____

_____

_____

_____

Self-Reflection:

- What did you learn about yourself this week?

Goals for Next Week:

- What are your goals for the upcoming week?

_____

_____

_____

_____

_____

_____

_____

_____

_____

Week 4

Achievements:

- What were your major achievements this week?

Challenges:

- What challenges did you face this week?

_____
_____
_____
_____
_____

- How did you overcome them?

_____
_____
_____
_____
_____
_____

Self-Reflection:

- What did you learn about yourself this week?

Goals for Next Week:

- What are your goals for the upcoming week?

_____

_____

_____

_____

_____

_____

_____

_____

_____

_____

Section IV: Monthly Reflections

Transitioning from Weekly to Monthly Reflections

It allows for deeper integration of insights and a more expansive perspective on personal growth. While weekly reflections offer a consistent touchpoint, shifting to a monthly practice provides the space to observe larger patterns, cycles, and progress over time. This longer interval encourages patience and prevents getting lost in the minutiae of daily or weekly fluctuations. Monthly reflections can create a more profound sense of accomplishment and allow for greater balance between introspection and action, fostering a more sustainable and aligned healing process for masculine energy.

Month 1

Overall Progress:

- How have you progressed towards your goals this month?

_____
_____
_____
_____

Self- Assessment:

- How do you feel about your mental, emotional, and physical health?

_____
_____
_____
_____
_____

Lessons Learned:

- What key lessons did you learn this month?

_____
_____
_____
_____
_____

Future Goals:

- Set new goals for the next month.

_____
_____
_____
_____

Month 2

Overall Progress:

- How have you progressed towards your goals this month?

_____
_____
_____
_____
_____

Self- Assessment:

- How do you feel about your mental, emotional, and physical health?

_____
_____
_____
_____
_____

Lessons Learned:

- What key lessons did you learn this month?

_____
_____
_____
_____

Future Goals:

- Set new goals for the next month.

_____
_____
_____
_____
_____

Month 3

Overall Progress:

- How have you progressed towards your goals this month?

_____

_____

_____

_____

Self- Assessment:

- How do you feel about your mental, emotional, and physical health?

_____

_____

_____

_____

Lessons Learned:

- What key lessons did you learn this month?

_____

_____

_____

_____

Future Goals:

- Set new goals for the next month.

_____

_____

_____

_____

Month 4

Overall Progress:

- How have you progressed towards your goals this month?

_____
_____
_____
_____
_____

Self- Assessment:

- How do you feel about your mental, emotional, and physical health?

_____
_____
_____
_____
_____

Lessons Learned:

- What key lessons did you learn this month?

_____

_____

_____

_____

Future Goals:

- Set new goals for the next month.

_____

_____

_____

_____

Month 5

Overall Progress:

- How have you progressed towards your goals this month?

_____
_____
_____
_____
_____

Self- Assessment:

- How do you feel about your mental, emotional, and physical health?

_____
_____
_____
_____
_____

Lessons Learned:

- What key lessons did you learn this month?

_____
_____
_____
_____
_____

Future Goals:

- Set new goals for the next month.

_____
_____
_____
_____

Month 6

Overall Progress:

- How have you progressed towards your goals this month?

_____
_____
_____
_____
_____

Self- Assessment:

- How do you feel about your mental, emotional, and physical health?

_____
_____
_____
_____
_____

Lessons Learned:

- What key lessons did you learn this month?

_____
_____
_____
_____

Future Goals:

- Set new goals for the next month.

_____
_____
_____
_____

Month 7

Overall Progress:

- How have you progressed towards your goals this month?

_____
_____
_____
_____
_____

Self- Assessment:

- How do you feel about your mental, emotional, and physical health?

_____
_____
_____
_____
_____

Lessons Learned:

- What key lessons did you learn this month?

_____
_____
_____
_____

Future Goals:

- Set new goals for the next month.

_____
_____
_____
_____

Month 8

Overall Progress:

- How have you progressed towards your goals this month?

_____
_____
_____
_____
_____

Self- Assessment:

- How do you feel about your mental, emotional, and physical health?

_____
_____
_____
_____
_____

Lessons Learned:

- What key lessons did you learn this month?

_____

_____

_____

_____

Future Goals:

- Set new goals for the next month.

_____

_____

_____

_____

Month 9

Overall Progress:

- How have you progressed towards your goals this month?

_____
_____
_____
_____

Self- Assessment:

- How do you feel about your mental, emotional, and physical health?

_____
_____
_____
_____
_____

Lessons Learned:

- What key lessons did you learn this month?

_____
_____
_____
_____

Future Goals:

- Set new goals for the next month.

_____
_____
_____
_____

Month 10

Overall Progress:

- How have you progressed towards your goals this month?

_____
_____
_____
_____
_____

Self- Assessment:

- How do you feel about your mental, emotional, and physical health?

_____
_____
_____
_____
_____

Lessons Learned:

- What key lessons did you learn this month?

_____

_____

_____

_____

Future Goals:

- Set new goals for the next month.

_____

_____

_____

_____

Month 11

Overall Progress:

- How have you progressed towards your goals this month?

_____
_____
_____
_____
_____

Self- Assessment:

- How do you feel about your mental, emotional, and physical health?

_____
_____
_____
_____
_____

Lessons Learned:

- What key lessons did you learn this month?

_____

_____

_____

_____

Future Goals:

- Set new goals for the next month.

_____

_____

_____

_____

Month 12

Overall Progress:

- How have you progressed towards your goals this month?

_____

_____

_____

_____

_____

Self- Assessment:

- How do you feel about your mental, emotional, and physical health?

_____

_____

_____

_____

_____

Lessons Learned:

- What key lessons did you learn this month?

_____

_____

_____

_____

_____

Future Goals:

- Set new goals for the next month.

_____

_____

_____

_____

_____

Section V: Guided Exercises

Reconnect Your Inner Warrior and Protector

Tap into a deep reservoir of strength, resilience, and courage that resides within. This inner warrior embodies the ability to face challenges head-on with determination and assertiveness, while your protector aspect is the guardian of your values, boundaries, and loved ones. By reawakening this energy, you reclaim your sense of purpose and leadership, ready to defend what matters most with clarity and honor. It is about standing tall, rooted in your core, knowing that you have the power to navigate adversity with calm confidence and unwavering commitment to your principles.

Exercise 1: Mindfulness Meditation

Here are Step-by-Step Guided Prompts for mindful meditation, designed to help restore masculine energy by enhancing traits such as focus, strength, confidence, and grounding. This guided meditation incorporates mindfulness techniques backed by scientific research.

Step 1: Set Your Intention

- Close your eyes and take a deep breath. In your mind, silently state your intention: 'I am here to reconnect with my inner strength, clarity, and purpose.' Allow this intention to settle into your mind, creating a focused and determined energy."

Step 2: Ground Yourself

- "Sit comfortably with your feet firmly on the ground. Imagine roots growing from the soles of your feet, anchoring you deep into the earth. Feel the stability and support of the ground beneath you, providing a strong foundation. With each breath, feel yourself becoming more grounded, more connected to the earth, steady and unshakable."

Step 3: Diaphragmatic Breathing

- "Place one hand on your belly and the other on your chest. Inhale deeply through your nose, allowing your belly to expand fully as you breathe in. Hold for a moment, then slowly exhale through your mouth, feeling your belly fall. Repeat this deep, diaphragmatic breathing for a few cycles. With each breath, you're activating your inner power, calming your mind, and enhancing your focus."

Step 4: Visualization of Masculine Archetypes

•"With your eyes still closed, imagine yourself standing tall, embodying a figure of strength and confidence. Visualize yourself as a powerful warrior, a wise leader, or a protector. See yourself facing challenges with calm determination, leading with authority, and standing firm in your convictions. Notice the feeling of strength and assertiveness that begins to rise within you."

Step 5: Body Scan with Focus on Core

• Prompt: "Now, shift your focus to your body. Starting from the top of your head, slowly scan down through your body. When you reach your abdomen, focus on your core, the center of your power. Visualize a warm, glowing ball of energy in your core. With each breath, feel this energy growing stronger, radiating confidence, strength, and willpower throughout your entire being. Stay here for a few moments, connecting deeply with this powerful energy."

Step 6: Mindful Movement

- "Now, slowly begin to move your body. If you're sitting, gently stretch your arms overhead, feeling the length and strength in your body. Stand up mindfully, feeling each foot connect with the ground. Move with purpose and intention, noticing how each movement feels strong, controlled, and deliberate. Allow this awareness to ground you even further in your masculine energy."

Step 7: Gratitude and Affirmation

- "Take a moment to express gratitude for this time you've taken to reconnect with yourself. Focus on one thing you are grateful for in your life. Now, repeat silently or aloud: 'I am strong. I am confident. I am grounded in my power.' Let these words resonate within you, reinforcing the masculine energy you've cultivated in this session."

Step 8: Closing and Reflection

- "Gently bring your awareness back to your surroundings. Wiggle your fingers and toes, and when you're ready, open your eyes. Take a moment to reflect on how you feel. Notice any changes in your energy, your mindset, or your body. Carry this renewed sense of strength, focus, and confidence with you throughout the rest of your day."

Additional Reflection:

After the meditation, take a few minutes to journal about your experience. Reflect on any insights, feelings, or shifts in your energy that occurred during the meditation. Use this as an opportunity to deepen your connection with your masculine energy.

PS: These guided Steps are designed to integrate mindfulness techniques that are scientifically linked to increased focus, confidence, and emotional balance, all of which contribute to restoring a strong, grounded masculine energy.

Exercise 2: Breathing Techniques

Restoring masculine energy through exercises that reduce stress and increase focus can be a powerful way to regain control, confidence, and mental clarity. These exercises will combine physical movement with mindfulness, enhancing both the mind and body's response to stress. This is a step-by-step guide to exercises that are scientifically proven to reduce stress and improve focus.

Step 1: Warm-Up with Dynamic Stretching

Objective: Activate your body and increase blood flow, preparing for focused movement.

- Why it works: Dynamic stretching prepares the muscles and nervous system for activity, improving circulation, flexibility, and mental readiness.

- How to do it:

    - Arm Circles: Stand with your feet shoulder-width apart. Rotate your arms in large circles forward and backward for 30 seconds each.

    - Hip Circles: Place your hands on your hips and rotate your hips in a circular motion, first clockwise and then counterclockwise for 30 seconds each.

    - Leg Swings: Hold onto a wall or sturdy object for balance. Swing one leg forward and backward in a controlled manner, then switch legs. Do 10 swings on each side.

Step 2: Box Breathing

Objective: Reduce stress and increase focus through controlled breathing.

- **Why it works:** Box breathing is a powerful breathing technique used to reduce stress and improve focus by calming the nervous system and bringing awareness to the present moment. Research shows it can lower cortisol levels and enhance cognitive function.
- **How to do it:**
    - Sit or stand in a comfortable position.
    - Inhale deeply through your nose for a count of four.
    - Hold your breath for a count of 4.
    - Exhale slowly through your mouth for a count of 4.
    - Hold the exhale for a count of 4.
    - Repeat this cycle for 2-5 minutes, focusing on the rhythm of your breath and feeling your body relax.

Step 3: Power Poses for Confidence

Objective: Boost testosterone levels and reduce cortisol through expansive, confident body postures.

- Why it works: Research suggests that holding a "power pose" for a few minutes can increase testosterone (associated with masculine energy) and reduce cortisol (the stress hormone), leading to increased confidence and focus.

- How to do it:

    - The Wonder Pose: Stand tall with your feet shoulder-width apart. Place your hands on your hips, elbows pointing out. Keep your chest open, head held high, and gaze forward. Hold this pose for 2 minutes.

    - Victory Pose: Stand tall with your feet shoulder-width apart. Raise your arms above your head in a "V" shape, as if celebrating a victory. Hold for 2 minutes while breathing deeply and visualizing yourself achieving your goals.

Step 4: High-Intensity Interval Training (HIIT)

Objective: Increase focus, release endorphins, and reduce stress through intense physical activity.

- Why it works: HIIT workouts combine short bursts of intense exercise with rest periods, which can improve cardiovascular health, boost mood, and sharpen mental focus. Research shows that this type of exercise can reduce anxiety and stress while increasing endorphin levels, leading to enhanced feelings of well-being.

- How to do it:

    - Perform the following exercises in intervals of 20 seconds of intense work, followed by 10 seconds of rest. Repeat each exercise for 3 rounds:

    1. Jump Squats: Lower into a squat position, then jump up explosively, landing softly and returning to the squat position.

    2. Push-Ups: Perform push-ups at a steady pace, engaging your core and keeping your body straight.

3. Mountain Climbers: Start in a plank position. Bring one knee towards your chest, then quickly switch legs in a running motion.

4. Burpees: From a standing position, squat down, place your hands on the floor, jump your feet back into a plank position, perform a push-up, jump your feet back in, and explosively jump up.

• Rest for 1 minute between rounds. The entire HIIT session should last about 10 minutes

Step 5: Yoga for Strength and Flexibility

Objective: Enhance focus, reduce stress, and restore masculine energy through mindful movement.

- Why it works: Yoga integrates breath control, physical postures, and meditation, making it effective for reducing stress, improving flexibility, and restoring mental focus. Yoga has been shown to reduce stress hormones and improve strength, flexibility, and overall body awareness.

- How to do it:

  - Warrior I Pose: Stand tall with your feet about 3-4 feet apart. Turn your right foot forward and your left foot at a 45-degree angle. Bend your right knee and raise your arms overhead, keeping your hips square. Hold for 30 seconds, then switch sides.

  - Warrior II Pose: From Warrior I, rotate your hips and torso to the side, extend your arms parallel to the ground, and gaze over your front hand. Hold for 30 seconds, then switch sides.

Step 6: Cool Down with Progressive Muscle Relaxation (PMR)

Objective: Reduce residual stress by systematically relaxing each muscle group.

- Why it works: PMR helps reduce muscle tension and stress by intentionally tensing and then releasing muscles. Studies show that this technique can significantly lower anxiety and promote relaxation.

- How to do it:

    - Find a comfortable seated or lying position.

    - Start with your toes: tense them for 5 seconds, then release. Move up your body, tensing and relaxing your calves, thighs, abdomen, chest, arms, hands, shoulders, and finally, your face.

    - As you relax each muscle group, focus on the sensation of tension leaving your body, and take slow, deep breaths throughout.

Step 7: Reflection and Journaling

Objective: Solidify the mental benefits of the exercises through mindful reflection.

- Why it works: Reflection and journaling help reinforce positive changes by engaging the brain's cognitive processes. This practice promotes self-awareness and helps you track your progress in stress reduction and focus enhancement.

- How to do it:

    - After your exercise session, take a few minutes to reflect on how you feel. Ask yourself:

    - How has my stress level changed?

    - How do I feel in terms of focus and mental clarity?
    - How connected do I feel to my inner strength and masculine energy?

    - Write down any insights, thoughts, or feelings that come up during your reflection.

Additional Tips:

1. Consistency: Incorporate these exercises into your routine 3-4 times a week for lasting benefits. Consistency will help you maintain reduced stress levels and increased focus over time.

2. Sleep and Nutrition: Complement your exercise routine with good sleep hygiene and a balanced diet. Rest and proper nutrition are key to restoring energy and overall well-being.

By consistently engaging in these exercises, you'll not only reduce stress but also cultivate a focused, powerful, and balanced masculine energy.

Create a vision board on these 5 Topics

Career & Business Success

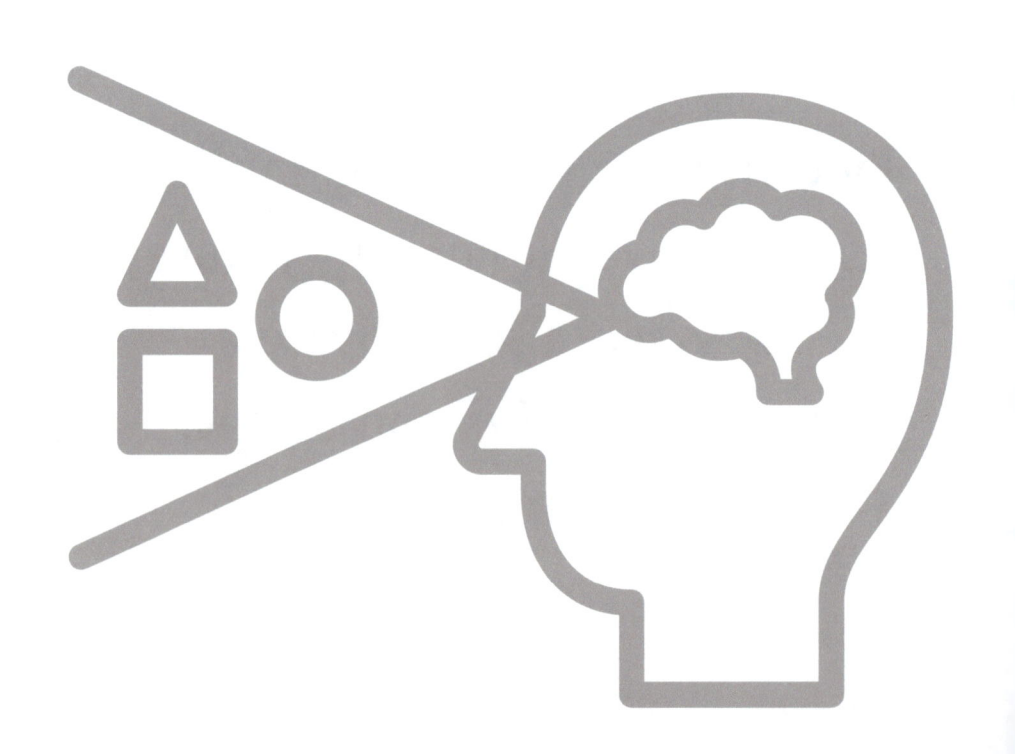

Health & Wellness

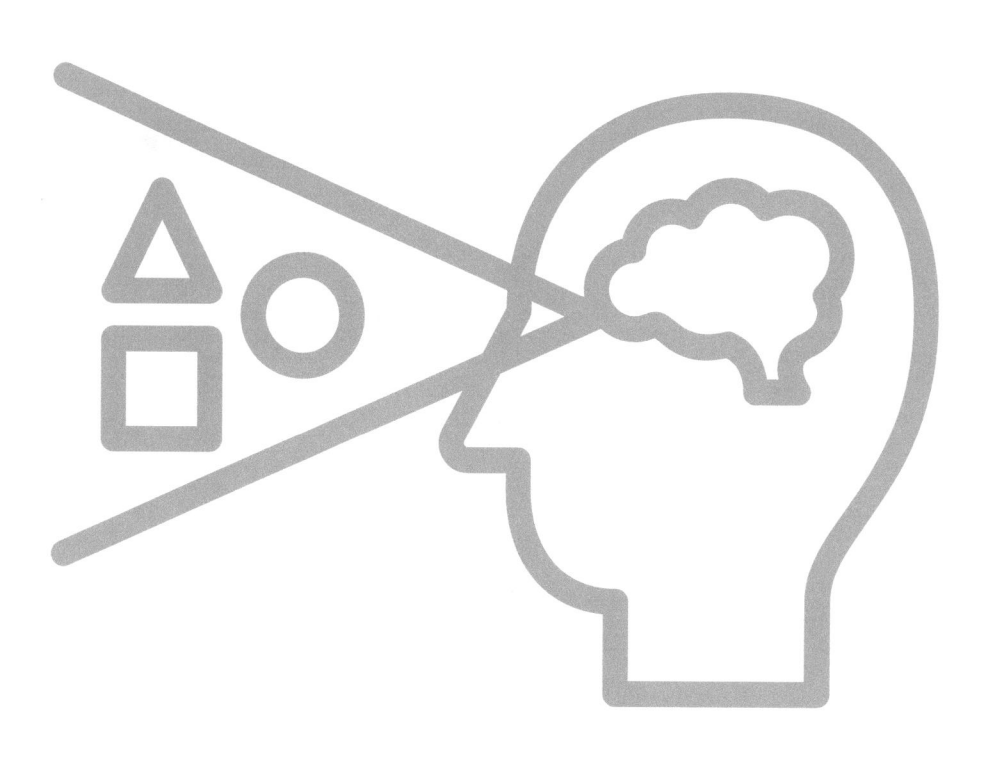

Travel & Adventure

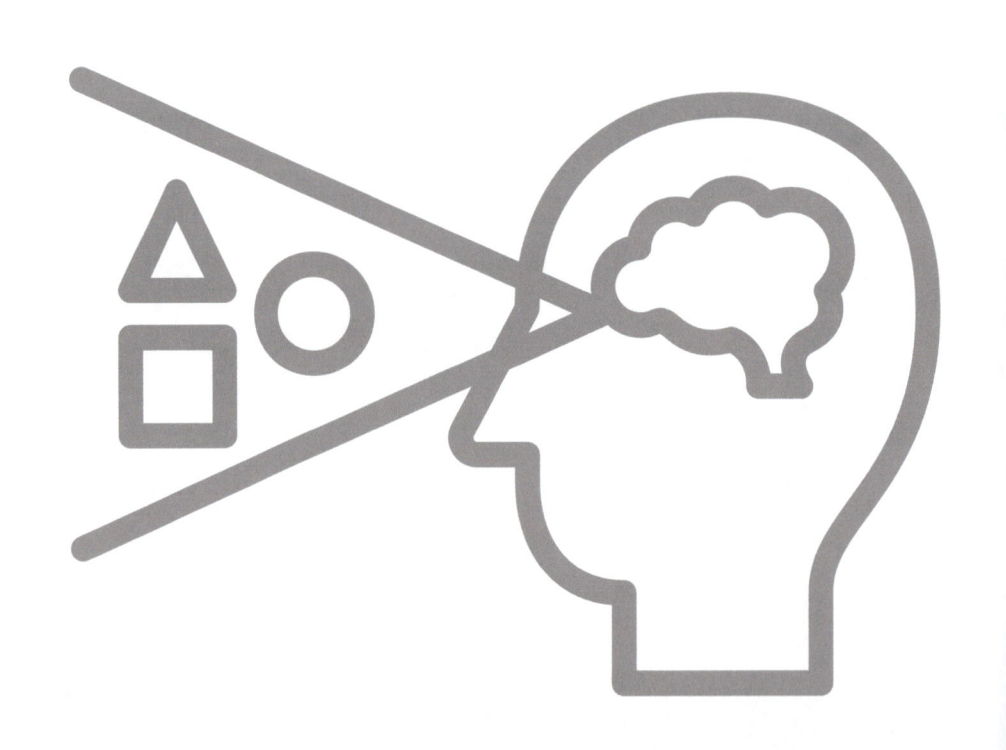

Personal Growth

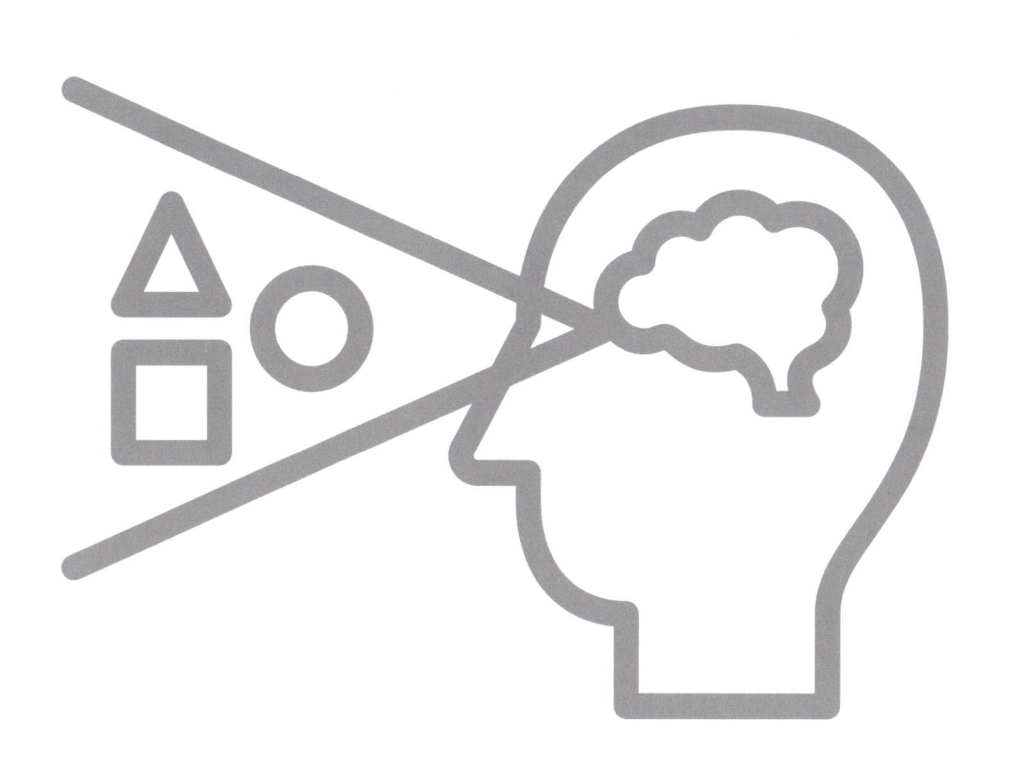

Family & Relationships

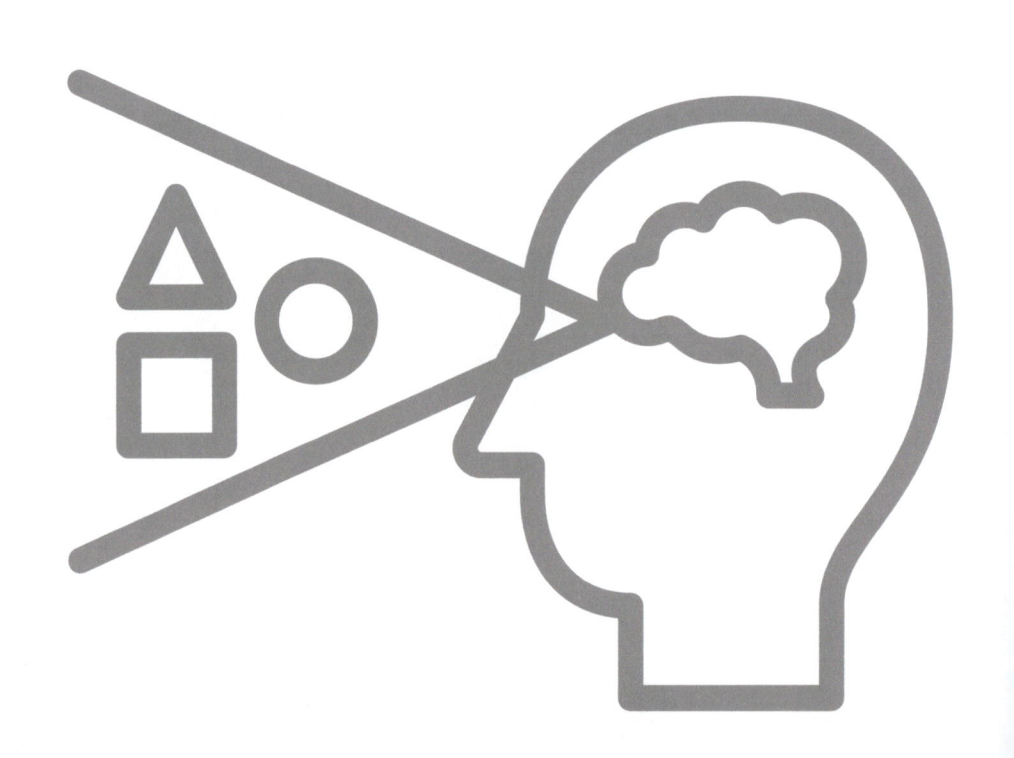

Gratitude Practice

Gratitude plays a powerful role in restoring masculine energy by grounding it in purpose and connection. When a being practices gratitude, they shift from a mindset of scarcity and stress to one of abundance and appreciation, helping them to reclaim their inner strength and sense of direction. Gratitude fosters humility and encourages a deeper connection to the present moment, which can reinvigorate the natural assertiveness and confidence that are central to masculine energy. By recognizing and valuing what is already present in their life, a being can channel their energy more constructively, fostering a balance between strength and vulnerability, and ultimately leading to a more centered and empowered expression of masculinity.

Here are three gratitude affirmation prompts focused on restoring masculine energy:

-I am grateful for:

_____

_____

_____

-I am thankful for:

_____

_____

_____

-I Love:

_____

_____

_____

Self-Compassion

Self-compassion is a vital tool for restoring masculine energy, as it allows a being to embrace their imperfections with kindness and understanding, rather than harsh judgment. By being gentle with yourself, you tap into a nurturing energy that balances the often intense drive of the masculine. This connection to self-compassion softens rigidity, creating space for growth and healing. It also bridges the gap between masculine and feminine energies, as the feminine encourages emotional openness, intuition, and receptivity. When a being integrates self-compassion, they harmonize their assertiveness with empathy, blending the masculine's strength with the feminine's emotional depth. This union fosters a more balanced, holistic expression of true self.

Here are a few exercises that help connect the masculine to the feminine, fostering self-compassion and restoring balanced masculine energy:

1. Mindful Journaling: Reflecting on Strength and Vulnerability

- Practice: Set aside 10-15 minutes daily to journal about moments where you've demonstrated strength, alongside moments where you've felt vulnerable. Reflect on how both experiences have shaped you positively.

- Goal: This exercise helps balance masculine strength with feminine vulnerability, fostering self-compassion by acknowledging and embracing both sides of your experience.

2. Heart-Centered Meditation

- Practice: Spend 10 minutes focusing on your heart center. Visualize warmth and light radiating from your heart, expanding throughout your body. With each breath, repeat affirmations like "I honor my strength" and "I embrace my sensitivity."

- Goal: This meditation bridges masculine focus with feminine emotional awareness, encouraging self-compassion through heart-centered energy.

3. Balanced Action and Rest

- Practice: Alternate between periods of focused action (masculine energy) and intentional rest or self-care (feminine energy). For example, after completing a task, take time to stretch, breathe, or meditate.

- Goal: This exercise teaches you to value both productivity and rest, balancing masculine drive with feminine nurturing, which promotes self-compassion by preventing burnout.

4. Compassionate Dialogue with Yourself

- Practice: When you're self-critical, pause and imagine speaking to yourself as you would to a loved one. Use kind, encouraging words, focusing on understanding rather than judgment.

- Goal: This exercise merges the masculine desire for self-improvement with the feminine quality of nurturing, helping to create a compassionate inner dialogue.

5. Creative Expression through Movement

- Practice: Engage in a physical activity that blends structure with fluidity, such as yoga, tai chi, or dance. Focus on how your body feels during the movement, and allow yourself to express emotions through it.

- Goal: This exercise connects masculine energy's focus and discipline with feminine energy's creative and expressive flow, fostering self-compassion through the embodiment of both energies.

By integrating these exercises into your routine, you can harmonize masculine and feminine energies, cultivating a more balanced and compassionate approach to life.

Closing

Embracing the Sacred Masculine

As we come to the end of this journey, let us remember that restoring the sacred masculine is not a single act but a continuous process of growth, reflection, and integration. It requires us to honor the deep wisdom within ourselves and to balance strength with vulnerability, action with reflection, and power with compassion.

In embracing this journey, we reclaim our connection to the divine masculine, recognizing that it is both a personal and collective responsibility. This path calls us to lead with integrity, protect with love, and stand firm in our truth while allowing space for others to do the same.

May this be the beginning of a new era in which the sacred masculine is fully awakened and harmonized within us all, guiding us toward a future of balance, wholeness, and unity.

With courage and grace, we move forward.

Made in the USA
Columbia, SC
14 September 2024